Cities Use Electricity

Electricity makes the lights go.

Electricity makes the clock go.

Electricity makes the bus go.

SLOW VEHICLE

NaVYa

Electricity makes the tram go.

9

Electricity makes the lift go.

11

Electricity makes the escalator go.

13

Electricity makes the car go.

Electricity makes this go too.